EXHALE AGAIN

Exhale Again

POEMS

by

ANDREA CLADIS

Adelaide Books
New York / Lisbon
2020

EXHALE AGAIN
a collection of poems by
Andrea Cladis

Copyright © Andrea Cladis
Cover design: Adelaide Books LLC
Cover image: Andrea Cladis

Published by Adelaide Books, New York / Lisbon
adelaidebooks.org

Editor-in-Chief
Stevan V. Nikolic

All rights reserved. No part of this book may be reproduced in any manner whatsoever without written permission from the author except in the case of brief quotations embodied in critical articles and reviews.

For any information, please address Adelaide Books
at info@adelaidebooks.org
or write to:
Adelaide Books LLC
244 Fifth Ave. Suite D27
New York, NY, 10001

ISBN: 978-1-952570-28-5

Printed in the United States of America

Dedication

Exhale Again is dedicated to the many acquaintances in my life who have taught me what it means to breathe in after heartache and exhale into new love. To my family and friends who have lifted me up and given me endless affirmation when I could not find it on my own, this collection is for you. And to the canine companions that have blessed my life – Sox, Chip, Dale, Kody, and Zoey, and Moka – your quiet, unconditionally loving, playful spirits have given me rest and inner peace in the lonely, dark hours of my life wherein I forgot what it was to stop, to listen, to lean in, and to just breathe.

To my husband, Matthew, for routinely teaching me how to breathe in and breathe out. For loving me so deeply that I have become comfortable enough to exhale in this life once again. For teaching me how to fully let go of that which does not serve my heart or nourish my soul. For loving me enough to make necessary sacrifices that have enabled me to continue the practice of writing. For encouraging me to devote myself to that which fuels my being and resonates within my heart. For holding my hand and allowing me to stop long enough to absorb the hidden beauty of this world. For your imagination and humor that cultivate new avenues of my personal curiosity. Many of the poems contained within this collection were originally drafted in the year of anticipation leading up to our September 22, 2018 wedding. In that time, my heart was renewed in the truth of lasting love and my desire to share the assurance and affirmation of our growing love together became abundantly clear. Matthew, I am most thankful for you and for the persistent, empowering gift of knowing what it feels like to be wholly known and unapologetically loved in this life.

Acknowledgements

A special thank you to the faculty and staff at Fairfield University who helped formatively shape my vision as an artist during my graduate school experience. To Karen Osborn for your wit, patience, and keen sense of perception in guiding me towards poets of like mind. To Baron Wormser, for teaching me distinct ways to enter into the life of a poem and to embody the experience of creation. Baron, your continued poetic wisdom in helping me to learn the value of word economy and to appreciate the careful construction of a poem's soundscape has been a guiding light for my poetry. To each and every faculty member who led engaging workshops or interactive seminars that challenged my poetic craft and gave me the courage to pursue the creative arts for the rest of my life, I thank you.

    Lastly, I thank my **Father in Heaven** for the miraculous gift of living in this world and sharing in His abundant creation. After every prayer, I continue to exhale deeply into the grace and knowledge of your life-giving love for us. **May the words I write forever bring you glory.**

About This Collection

Attempting to capture all stages of emotional grief and triumph, *Exhale Again* centers around the power of love to heal, the will of the mind to persist, and the tenacity of the human spirit to hold onto faith in all circumstances. The ecstasy of love realized and the analysis of the peril that exists within the human condition provide breadth to this collection. Stylistically dynamic, this collection includes amorous anecdotes revealing the desire of the human heart to remain in love alongside the oft harsh reality that hope deterred, though painful, can be a great source of renewal. Exhale Again is a mixed format poetry collection most heavily laden with lyric poetry interspersed with poems of varied pentameter and set form poems including haikus, sonnets, and limericks intended to reignite our collective belief in hope, while exploring what it is in this life that makes us feel whole, worthy, respected, and alive.

Contents

PART I: BREATHE

Haiku Triad #1   *13*

His Smile   *14*

Blush: The Lover's Meet   *15*

Seen   *16*

My Comfort, My Joy   *17*

My Refuge Here   *20*

The Gift   *21*

Twilight Harbor   *22*

PART II: HONOR

Haiku Triad #2   *27*

Love Burns Eternal   *28*

Unsalted Secrets   *29*

Admiration   *30*

Love Cascades   *32*

I Love You When   *33*

Spirit in the Sky   *34*

Behind the Altar Kiss   *35*

"I do"   *38*

PART III: INQUIRE

Haiku Triad #3 *41*

The Fruits of Lost Affection *42*

Cobblestone Street Conversation *45*

Looking After Time *47*

Presence *49*

Mystical Moonshine *50*

Photograph *52*

Loving You is the Mystery *53*

PART IV: EXHALE

Haiku Triad #4 *57*

Anxiety *58*

His Patience is my Peace *60*

Restless in Love *61*

Keeper of Secrets *62*

Holy Art Thou Underwear *63*

Lighthouse *64*

Lover's Limerick *65*

I am that which I AM *66*

About the Author *71*

Part I
BREATHE

HAIKU TRIAD #1

Call it a gifting.
The placid morning takes breath.
You saw her beauty.

        "Sing louder," he said.
        I need to hear your heart speak.
        Voice is who you are.

                Watch the evening sun.
                Does the horizon deceive?
                Witness her story.

Andrea Cladis

HIS SMILE

Beaming, his eyes -
        Brightened, his face.
The day I first saw his smile.

I wished to make it last forever,
Is happiness ever out of style?

Laughing, his dimples -
        Impish, his cheeks.
I stared not knowing why.

I fell in love with him, asking -
Would there have to be a goodbye?

When he smiles, the sun finds the moon.
        When he smiles life's sweet, tender perfume.
           My heart bubbles beyond.
And when he smiles just because he looked at me,
        I see God's adoring hand in
           our story.

BLUSH: THE LOVER'S MEET

Rouge upon her cheeks
Warmth swelling her hands
Eyebrows raised, sparkling eyes –
    In awe.

                      Mellow mousse holding his brunette hair
                              Tension lifting his shoulders
                                  Eyes entranced with what
                                        He saw.

Thoughts dancing into truth
Queries resolved without words
The cautious gaze left her
    Glowing.

                    Fixed stares admiring purity in beauty
                            Daydreaming in brilliant color
                            Masculine confidence he felt
                                    In knowing—

He was her man. She was his girl.
Joining their hands, long-awaited like a fresh pearl
revealing the ivory gem within.
Precious, slowly growing, polished as royalty, treasured, worthy
well beyond its home.
She blushed into the
new love

        They owned.

Andrea Cladis

SEEN

His eyes reflected,
The first time that I met him.
My hidden story.

MY COMFORT, MY JOY

The crowded coffee shop
in early spring

was where I first met
the gentleman who
one day would make

me sing.

Unassuming were his ways as
He greeted me –
nothing overstated like
other men trying to impress with

fancy watches and well-pressed money.

Carefully he spoke of the bold colors
of my blouse.

His lips in a partial smile, I knew this
was the boy I'd take to
my parent's house.

Andrea Cladis

Roasted vanilla grounds delighted my nose
as I squinted into the sun.
Open windows, my warming face,
Praying to God my mascara wouldn't run.

His silhouette a shadow from my sunlit view,
Handsome, his distinct jawline was watching -
Minty, his cologne was taunting,
His V-neck tee, a soft sun-washed blue.

Playing with a polished penny atop my lap
I dropped it to avert my eyes and
heard the barista clap,
    "Your order is ready!"

He bent down to pick up
my penny.

He said, his voice a protective levee,
    "Will you please switch sides of the table?
        Sit over here, it's the least I am able."
My penny perched next to my coffee,
I didn't know why he only bought one -
His forehead perspired, now taking on the bright light,
Our sunny romance had only just begun.

The penny looked at me and then over at him.
He queried, "Are you okay?"
The sun at my back, his dark, calming eyes,
Admiring and slim.

My comfort was his joy.
Never have I forgotten that moment of
Frothy coffee,
    Daring sunshine, and
        Sweet, sweet chivalry.

MY REFUGE HERE

Five years ago I met you –
You came and changed my life.
Five years ago you showed me a world past pain and strife.

I came with a fragile heart,
Hurt, hollow, timid towards love.
I came with an independent spirit, feisty or "fine,"
                                         but lonely, ever-longing for love.

You drew me in patiently - kind eyes and a gentle hand,
Breaking down stubborn walls,
You've proven I'm worth loving, despite tears, stumbles or falls.

You taught me love must be fought for –
No matter what the cost.
You've held my hand and opened my heart,
                       Reminding me that I will never again be lost.

You've believed in my dreams.
You've held me steadfast.
You've shown me that together we're building a love that will last.

Leading, loving, and lending an ear,
With a watchful eye, I'm always sheltered from fear.
Addlepated I'm not when your presence is near,
Resting eyes, rhythmic breath, my refuge is here.

THE GIFT

Call it a gifting –
The placid morning takes breath
Witness its beauty.

TWILIGHT HARBOR

The clouds today
shaded my sight as I
listened for
the cadence.

Misty, climbing,
Amorphous,
White.

His heart pulses two times too fast –
loops upward to try
               again.
What might!
Falling gently into
       place.
Soft winds through crusted leaves try to re-create.

Cloudy days when the rains release
the pitter patter,
Plop, plot of drops
       So heavy
       So warm
       So unassuming,
Accumulate.

EXHALE AGAIN

My heart tells a story much the same,
questioning what's right,
answering what's wrong -

The purple sun filters into the horizon
I do not wish for the dawn.

Humming to its beat.
I can't savor this sleep.
Relentless
hearts searching,
        waiting to be one.

The clouds still carry our rain.
        We breathe.

At twilight,
        We find the harbor.

Part II
HONOR

HAIKU TRIAD #2

If I only knew
The heartache of tomorrow
Would last forever.

                Growing up I thought
                The bruises, blisters would heal
                I can still see them.

                                Where is it you find
                                The serum not for aging,
                                But for feeling whole?

Andrea Cladis

LOVE BURNS ETERNAL

He called me a *Flare*
A force that radiated –
Brightly Burning.

He called me a Flare
A light that flickers,
Long after dark.

He called me a Flare,
Unaware of the colorful passion
within my being.

He said, "Life is not the same
without your glow…"
But does he know the source
of its warmth?

A *Flare* only catches fire when love
Burns eternal.

EXHALE AGAIN

UNSALTED SECRETS

A tidal wave
that washes clean
Past debris –

Endless is his love for me.

The salt that heals,
carries the ocean's
Deepest secrets.

I am floating in his love that listens -

To the crest of
every new wave
and the salt that
sweetly stings
each wound.

I am free.

Andrea Cladis

ADMIRATION

He looked at me tonight in a way that reminded me
    I am more.
I am more than the young girl in an orange cotton sundress
    longing to be loved.
I am more than the times I have been
    bruised or mistreated.
I am more than the woman chasing
    scholarly degrees.

I am more than just a
    dancer, writer, creator, or teacher.
I am more than my successes and never less than
    my failures.
I am more than the arguments, more than the flaws, more than
the contradictory clause of
my life that
queried and rejected
my being.

I was more than worth
    The
       Wait.
I am more.

    For I am God's daughter and
      I am *his*
         Beloved.

Andrea Cladis

LOVE CASCADES – *A Petrarchan Sonnet*

Will you please have this dance with me?
One phrase of 32 counts is all that we'll need.
Take me in frame, I'll follow your lead.
Spontaneous your music, which sets my soul free.

The society tempo, the syncopated beat -
It was for me that you learned how to dance.
Given this moment again, would you still take the chance?
Your steady embrace, your smooth romance
Guiding the suede steps of my feet.

Softly we waltz as the music fades,
I lift my arm, a release – you twirl away.
With your close coil back into me, our love made new.
I lose my place as your curly brown hair cascades
I follow. The dimple on your back reminds, there's much I wish to say,
Hold onto me today, more tightly tomorrow,
Endlessly I wish only to have this dance with you.

I LOVE YOU WHEN

I love you
    in the morning.

I love you
        in the evening.

I love you
    in the moments between
        meaning.

I love you
    now.
And I'll love you
    when –

It begins
    and when it all ends.

The ocean's midnight waves
    echo his cry.

I'll love you until the end

        of forever.

Andrea Cladis

SPIRIT IN THE SKY

Sometimes when I fly
high above the clouds -
I think I spot an
angel floating
right on by.

The expanse of the forested
land below seems too much for
softly sprawling,
white-laced wings.

How do they choose where to go?

A frosty flash, a white-orange flare,
They trick the eyes –
Spirits weaving between cotton-pillowed pleas,
Decorating the sun-kissed skies.

When the plane descends
beneath the clouds,
I blink and fix my gaze.

The land below
will meet those marveled angels,
unknown to me -
all the inexplicable ways.

BEHIND THE ALTAR KISS

Give me reason to believe -
    This love will last forever.
Give me reason to believe -
        We chose the right endeavor.
When you kissed me at the altar -
    It was me whose feet did falter.
When you held me during grief's long cry -
        It was you who desperately wanted to try –

To paint and reassemble
    The unnamed anxiety which made me toil and tremble.

Give me reason to believe -
    This love is to be treasured.
Give me reason to believe -
        There's promise past the pleasure.
When our silken sheets are silent, singing
    And the echo of our wedding bells stop fast their ringing -
When I question, "What more can I ask of you?"
        When everything you've risked has made our love new.

Andrea Cladis

To feel your warmth
as I watch you sleep.
    I do not resent you.
But why don't I know how
    to want you?

Like a building fashioned to withstand hurricanes,
    The violet winds don't sway.
The assurance of your love –
Freely given
    every day.

Give me reason to believe -
When I knelt and kissed your forehead
    Your heart sounded softly, blushing red.
Give me reason to believe -
    I am beauty *seen*.
Like snow clasping onto the forest's branches
      as the winter sun tests their melting strength.
Give me reason to believe that daring hug of snow remains.

EXHALE AGAIN

The reason is I love you -
    I always have and will
The reason is I love you -
    Though oft you forget how,
        Through the snowclad branches,
Hidden and seeking my love,
    It is only you I see now.

The reason is I love you –
    Your heart chose mine to adore
Today, tomorrow, and evermore.
    Yes, my dear –
        I'm still here.
And always shall it be that I will love you -
        More.

Andrea Cladis

"I DO"

Lover's win hearts
and losers fail to keep them.
A vow, a pledge or promise,
won't be all we need then.

Today we say, "I do" and tomorrow
We are made new.
Through the eyes of our Father,
I'll continually learn to
Better love
You.

Part III
INQUIRE

HAIKU TRIAD #3

When he left, I cried.
Can I be happy alone?
I hear his whispers.

                Breath coils in the cold.
                They call it January.
                The stillness grows old.

                                Mistaken I was -
                                When I fell in love.
                              My heart was never returned.

Andrea Cladis

THE FRUITS OF LOST AFFECTION

I watched
the ripening bananas
day after day
green to yellow and
yellow to spotted brown.

He never ate them and I
became sick of their
soft, potassium-burning
weight upon my empty,
coffee-stained stomach.

Spotted brown to
a coil of darkened despair.

Would our love, untouched, also
whither and warp,

turn to brown?

I watched
the growing grapes
red and green
flouncing about
for nearly two weeks.

EXHALE AGAIN

I only ate a few bunches of
the supple plumpness they
no longer offered as
I learned where raisins come from.

Would our love,
also become dry
like the grapes that make

soured wine?

I watched the shrinking strawberries
cuddle into a wooly wrap
like a caterpillar
in the fall,
yet unmoving.

When I could no longer see their seeds,
I cradled them in my palms.
Caressing with my thumbs,
praying for life to return.

Would our love
also fade from red to gray?
Hiding like the hovering clouds
on an unforgiving winter day?

Andrea Cladis

Sit and scowl
Think and wonder
Question, is there more?

The fruit bowl offered little pleasure.
Bemused by its uncompromised dismay –
The fruit bowl held the most desperate
perfume of

unrelenting premonition.

Sugar-soaked gnats bobbed in the stationary air around a
softly frowning yellow pear.

The apple I cut had soggy seeds.

Perhaps the last fruit of which to share
is that of our rotting love still trying

to care.

EXHALE AGAIN

COBBLESTONE STREET CONVERSATION

A petticoat checkered with four prose buttons of memory –
One, the day her father left home.   Two, the way she grew up too soon.
Three, the play where death always wins.   Four, the May her father returned.

Hair tousled, loose amber curls
Her gray cloche hat hid a single red rose petal -
     her mother's funeral.

Rain boots tapping
on the puddles of
paused promises.
     Faded yellows, a fragmented family.

"It's May and the clouds are crying," she began.
     "It's May and…"
     "I miss her, too," he said. "My only love."
"There's flowers, Dad. Do you see them?"
     "They are beautiful, dear. As are you."
"The pinks, the whites, the blues…"
     "Your mother would have picked them all."

Looking down upon the troubled cobblestone street,
     she sighed.
"Why didn't you save her? My baby sister was inside."
     "The car was coming at us so fast. I had no control."

Andrea Cladis

The crinkles in his voice pleaded,
      "I'm so sorry, Catherine."

In the town at quarter to four,
umbrellas frowned, deep glossed navy.

Heaven's rains fell -
Dampening the flowers of every colored memory and
      Forgiveness.

LOOKING AFTER TIME

He said time is all we have to
                            give.
And time is all we have to
      lose.

He said time is all we have right
                            now.
And time is what you spent telling me to
      go.

He said time grants no offer of
                            return.
And time is unkind in the silence of
      moving space.

He said time ceases to pause when I ask
                                it to.
And time feels eternal when I am next
      to you.

He said time doesn't try to steal our
                                joy.
But time doesn't have to wait for my tease to make you
      Laugh.

Andrea Cladis

Who compels this time to pass?
While I'm still staring through the looking glass?

Patiently knowing
Cautiously aware -

I will never have enough of it
with you.

PRESENCE

Be here in this moment with me,
Stop the vapid stares from the others.

How do you see the world?
A screen is not alive, but you are.

Touch the Frasier Fur in winter,
Dust the feathery snow from your warm hands.

Taste the seeded watermelon, freshly sliced,
Its savory juices, cold and sweet.

Smell the grass of summer's scorching heat,
The wave of floral green.

Listen to the grains of sand on the beach at sunset.
Be alive with them.

Swirl into the wind as they do,
Flip flop towards the ocean's open mouth.

Feel the rain as it falls gently
Let the water caress your ears.

Look up!
Be present!
There's people here,
But there's glory
There.

Andrea Cladis

MYSTICAL MOONSHINE

I didn't know his name.
The shape of his shadowed frame
said, "Come."

Come closer.
I have a living wish for you.

The moon shone upon my slippers.
The wind ruffled my robe
Silken waves,
Unwanted sleep.
The cemetery home.

Come closer.

I moved towards the voice,
I think it was a man.
A whisper –

Dance until sunrise.

Moonlight spotlight
Twirling laughter
Summer night
Silken red robe -
Dancing.

EXHALE AGAIN

I moved closer.

Dance until sunrise.

Come closer.
Dance with me
                     until sunrise.

A slim silhouette,
A youthful man.

I mirrored the smoothness of his movement,
            the rhythm his own.

Maybe I never heard him.
Perhaps I never saw him.

         I'm certain that was the first time I met him.

       My grandfather,
            dancing until sunrise.

PHOTOGRAPH

Cameras Capture
    Distant emotions.
A flash of
Pivotal change.

Cameras Capture
    Speckled darkness.
A fury of
Magniloquent exchange.

Cameras Capture
    Candid glances
Jaunty, unaware, or strange.

Cameras Capture
    Lover's wish lists,
Not ready for this
Charade.

LOVING YOU IS THE MYSTERY

Each night when midnight falls upon
      my weary eyes,
I pray for you.

      I thank God for you.
      I ask for another day to
          learn to
      Love you.

The forehead kisses
The eyes that shade my breath
The touch of your gentle hands -

      Blissful on my skin.

If there's one poem,
I can't quite master,
It's the endless chase after,
      How?
          How can I tell you all the ways I love you,
              any faster?

When your lips find mine again,
They'll speak of the words still lost to my pen.

Part IV
EXHALE

HAIKU TRIAD #4

The needle through skin
Searching for a blue river
Couldn't find the vein.

                    Is laughter proper joy?
            When God doesn't smile right back?
                        Crying, is it sin?

                                        Crumpled leaves falling
                                        They will not return again
                                            Sideways to the wind.

ANXIETY

A tingle
        rustling up

stopping at my neck,
I can't take breath.

A blink,
        unnoticed.

Eyes open, rapidly tracking,
Mind's memory boxes stacking.

An alarm
        beeping

into the caverns of my hollow ears
the perpetual pulse has been present for years.

EXHALE AGAIN

A shudder
        radiating agony

through my right shoulder
Anguish for now I'm growing older.

A swelling
        panic

pacing away the pain is denied,

I fear right now I'm *too* alive.

Andrea Cladis

HIS PATIENCE IS MY PEACE

My mind is a constant storm
    winds of emotion,
memories morphing into
      thunderous noise,
Lost to loneliness.

Haunting obsessions like hail
    pestering the kettle-clay roof
      in early spring.

Lightning sparks new ideas –

Surging energy,
Endless motion.

      His Embrace is my calm.
      His Query is my quiet.
      His Patience is my peace.

The rainbow comes after the storm.

EXHALE AGAIN

RESTLESS IN LOVE

His heartbeat, a flicker
    gaining new strength.
It's out of place rhythm
      reminds the time in this life
travels too swiftly –
    and sometimes too slowly.

I fell asleep humming to
    its out of place beat –
The first thing I noticed
      about him is becoming
the one thing I can't
    live without.

I inhale, holding my breath,
    awaiting his exhale.
My head upon his chest –
      The flicker is quicker
and lighter
    in love.

KEEPER OF SECRETS

Provider of truth.
Healer of sordid sadness.
Vault of my secret.

HOLY ART THOU UNDERWEAR

A grand eruption
      A Volcanic force.
A vibration so intense.

I trembled.

Gripping sheets,
compelled to inflation
by fatal flatulence.

Parachute pants!
His holy boxers!

Can you believe, it's all one man?

I prayed into the building warmth,
    "Father! Thy will be done!"

Through the smoke cloud,
A gasp for clean air,
A glimmer of white!
I rolled over to kiss him and
that's why he made me his wife.

Andrea Cladis

LIGHTHOUSE

Noticeably mesmerized when he stares into
        a smile from my eyes.
Patiently delicate -
        His glance sets free my
            inner beauty.
We find tranquility.

When someone believes in loving you,
It emboldens you to love yourself, too.
        Searching and finding -
        Waiting and wanting,
        Leading and protecting.
My lighthouse illumines our shore.

LOVER'S LIMERICK

We wrote the most
        beautiful song.

Lover's lips unlocked,
        the call to belong.

The first verse was mine -
The chorus, divine.

Unceasing we pray, our music plays on.

Andrea Cladis

I AM THAT WHICH *I AM*

I am the beloved doctor's daughter -
Whose father died of cancer.
Whose supporting wife is pained by illness and want of perfection.
Whose son has been haunted by years of depression.
Medicine can't fix everything.

I am the righteous Christian woman.
I am the Chalice bearer at Church.
I don't always take communion.
Refusal of the wafer is deemed satanic.
I believe, but I don't always smile at my God.

I am the energetic fitness trainer
who plans, who helps, who bears
the burdens of those who can't find health.
I am the success of those who do.
I am the failure of those who don't.
I am a body, broken by repetitive injury.

I am the white woman perpetually called, "Privileged."
I am the white woman -
Alone in a bathroom stall
Forced to fit an image.

EXHALE AGAIN

I am the Greek woman.
Strong and Fierce and Present
Obliged to dote on men and
serve the patriarchy of a family
I often resent.

I am the academic, concealing achievement.
I am the writer, embittered by loneliness.

I am the rape victim who never spoke up.
I am the bruised memory
who was told if I wasn't pregnant,
for the man, that was luck.

I am the schoolteacher who
conforms to the rules.
I am the target of those who imbibe in
cruel fabrications,
gossiping about others.
My best friends are students, twenty years younger.

Andrea Cladis

I am the baker who
uses real sugar, real flour, all hail the gluten!
I am the high school barista who
made the wealthy housewives' lattes with full-fat milk,
not skim.
Their plastic waists and hips were far
too slim.

I am courage and
I am failure.

I am confidently sorrowful.

I am imperfection,
Chasing the gods of life's great order.

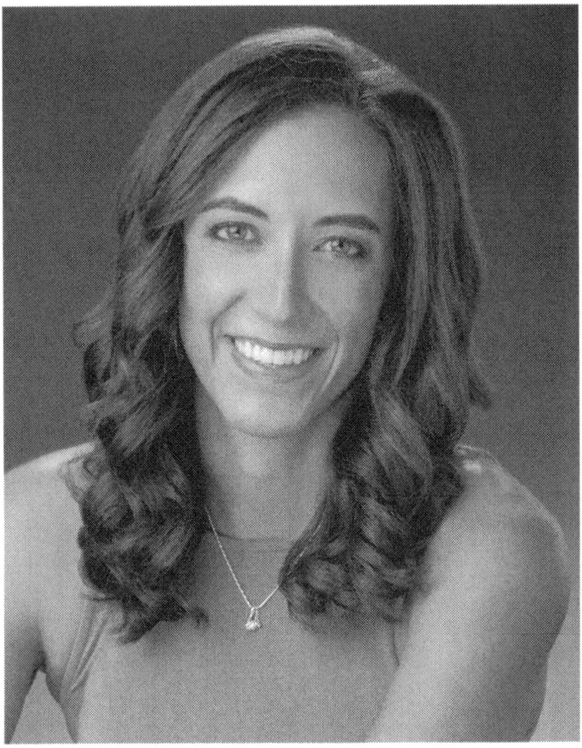

About the Author

Andrea Cladis Hodge holds an MFA in Writing from Fairfield University and is a Summa Cum Laude graduate of Elmhurst College with degrees in English Writing, Interdisciplinary Communications, French, and Secondary Education. She currently works as an English Writing Professor at Columbia College in Chicago, a freelance editor, writing consultant, and licensed fitness professional. She is an Advisory Board Member for Cambridge Scholars Publishing and has been published by SAGE Academic, NOVA Science Publishers, and several print and online publications including The Greek Star and Patch.com. Her writing has been described as "emotive, yet brazen, seasoned with thinly veiled cynicism, and a hint of sarcasm." She is the author of the memoir, *Tatsimou, Hold On!*, the Christian nonfiction books, *Finding the Finish Line* and *Fearless Stride*, and the poetry collection, *Forgotten Coffee*. In addition to writing, Andrea loves to inspire others through high energy dance and fitness classes. When she is not writing or teaching, you will find her cooking, reading, competing in triathlons and marathons, spending time with her family, and serving at her church. For more information about her books and freelance writing services, visit www.tanagerwriting.com. You can also connect with her via Instagram: @writer_andi_hodge or on Facebook: @WriterAndi (Andrea Cladis, Author).

Made in the USA
Middletown, DE
20 November 2024